SHE, A BLUEPRINT

SHE, A BLUEPRINT

MICHELLE NAKA PIERCE text

SUE HAMMOND WEST image

She, A Blueprint published by BlazeVOX [books]
Copyright © 2011 Michelle Naka Pierce and Sue Hammond West

Printed in the United States of America
Cover art: Sue Hammond West
Cover design: HR Hegnauer
First Edition
ISBN: 978-1-60964-060-6
Library of Congress Control Number: 2011905690

BlazeVOX [books]
76 Inwood Place
Buffalo, NY 14209
editor@blazevox.org

publisher of weird little books

BlazeVOX [books]

blazevox.org

2   4   6   8   0   9   7   5   3   1

for Ronnie and Bhanu

for Rex and Jivan

ACKNOWLEDGMENTS

Grateful acknowledgment to Drew Kunz, editor of Tir Aux Pigeons, who published an excerpt of this project as a chapbook: *As Transient as Square or Inside 32* (2008).

Appreciation to the editors of *American Letters and Commentary*, *Bombay Gin*, *Fact-Simile*, *Foursquare*, *Inquiring Mind*, *Mandorla*, *Monkey Puzzle*, *Sous Rature*, *Trickhouse*, and *Upstairs at Duroc* (France), where some of this work previously appeared, sometimes in earlier versions.

Thanks also to Gabrielle Civil, HR Hegnauer, Michiko Masuda Pierce, Chris Pusateri, and Laura Seligman for their support. Finally, much gratitude to Geoffrey Gatza.

CONTENTS

Gordon Matta-Clark   *Anarchitecture attempts to solve no problem.*

Pamela M. Lee   *A place that is an "interruption" or a "movement space" is a liminal space.*

Bhanu Kapil   *[I]n the process of carving out a territory,…we also carve out something like a body for ourselves. So this dual operation of territory and body is produced simultaneously.*

[Lot 32]

just so.

[LOT 1]

Inside is outside not outside, not even with glass. A single continuous curve, simply one boundary. Not square or rectangle, not in little places. Not in neglect and abandon. Not in chimney, not flue and vent please. Single door single door single keyhole door sight. A sweet floor and not less noisy than cedar and more garden than vinyl and nearly well varnished by things just so. Please, she said, shade. It is necessary and beside the large sort is sky. Every way wind. Please prune near the house. It is not the same day today. This is. Which makes a space, which makes a house inside town or city. Inside little boxes made of signs of things to come. Display dark. In a stream of recollection, new hands. Not to be narrowly. Not to be just so.

Parcel A. On The Verge Of Collapse,
Mark The Height. Preserve Her Migrant Square.

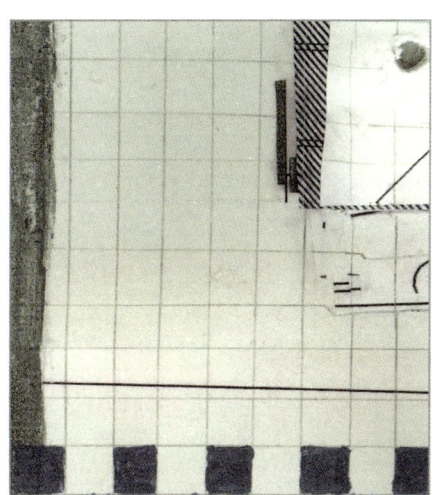

[LOT __]

CYLINDER:	A STREAM OF URINE DISTURBED	
	BY THE EXERCISE OF KEGEL	
	PERIOD	EXPULSION

14

[LOT 2]

Or she says. These might not be needed (planks, wires, load-bearing walls). Bigger than. Smaller than. She puts things in the medicine chest, now recessed. Hidden behind mirror. Hidden behind face, wrinkle (growing into crevice) on the forehead. Hidden behind plucked chin hairs, discolored skin or blemish. Current homes omit these nooks. Sometimes the cabinet opens. She wants to look inside. She wants to see the interior of containers: often orange or sepia. She says, open the inside of inside of safety. She says, open the cylinder of space. Her desire, worn.

Note: Load-bearing does not refer to an unattainable waist/hip ratio.

[LOT 3]

She demanded to see the inside of the outside. The slit between the two. Determine whether the home was sound or an imposter with no walls, actually walls, but no foundation, actually foundation but no coverage. The cut wide open and the neighbors see everything. The cut wide, but not open, and the neighbors hear chainsaws, stairs split in half. How to move from first floor to second floor and back. With eaves off their eaves on display. The attic in hallucination is only contextually an attic. The attic came through the window. See dust mite. See termite. See this. She attempts to construct a primary semblance of domestic reality. The blueprint was set adrift where cerulean meets ink. Image appears through tracing, washed in running water, then dried. Loaded with right angles and dotted lines where ingress and egress are permitted.

Parcel B. She Rises Into Ruin As She Fills In The Diagram.

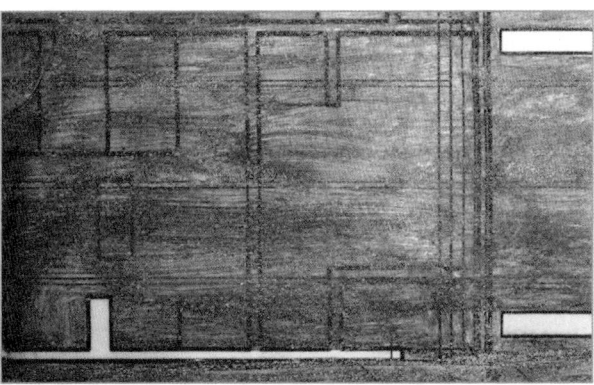

Legend

Slit: Suture After Caesarian. No Use Of Electrical Wire.

[LOT 4]

Take back the domicile—the bolster from the cotton, the floorboard from the maple, the countertop from the granite or the sweet. Take back the chair rail, make it vertical and chaste. Or the fixture from the water. Take back the damp, the wet. And make it transparent. If the private were taken away from the private and the public taken away from the public and the space between disappeared. Take back the design, the ruined carpet, the mousetrap, the night. If the inside were outside and the outside the inside structure of this. Passage.

Legend

Passage Scale: A Foot Equals The Length Between Wrist & Elbow.

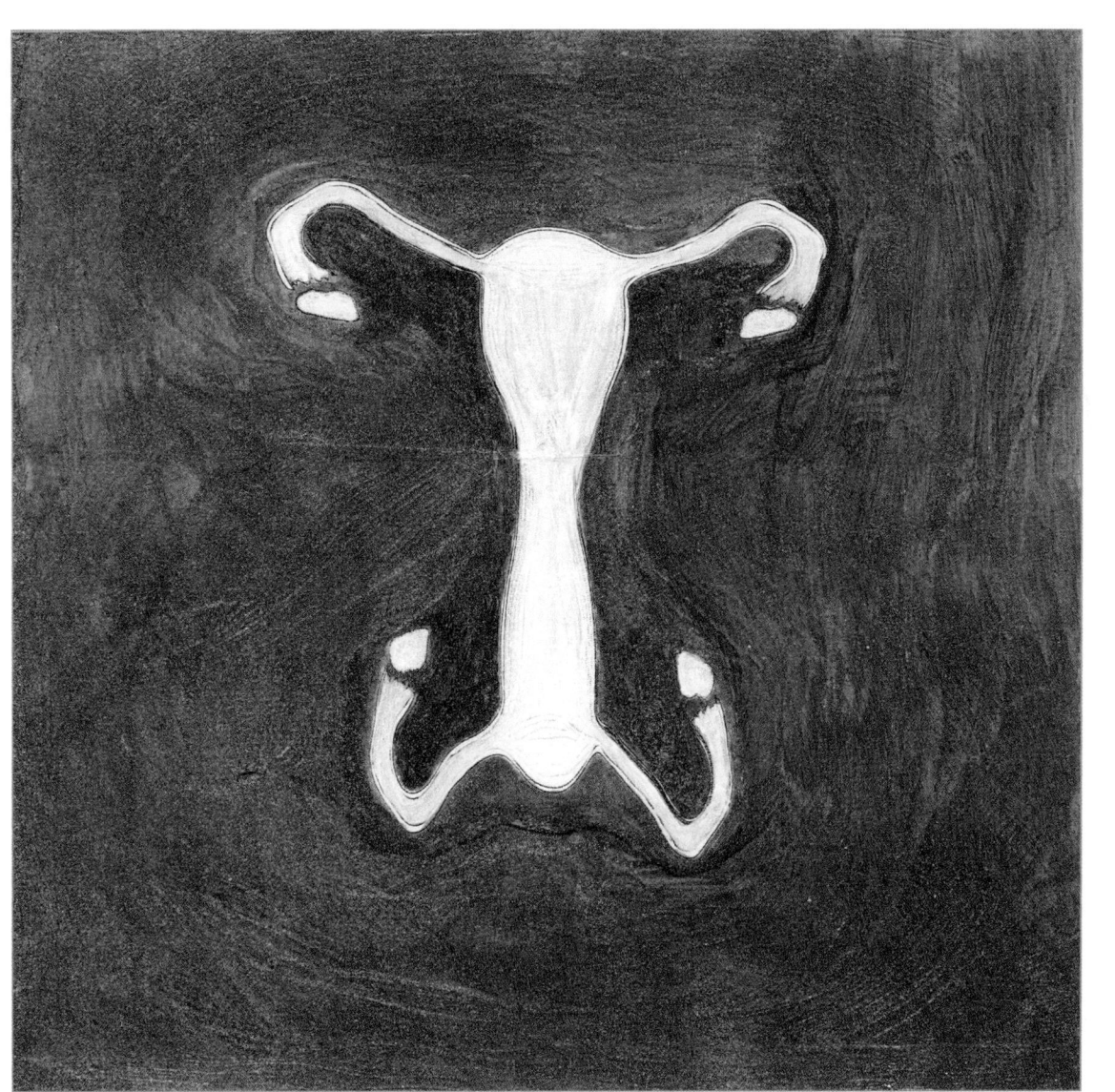

CUT (1)

A glass curve is a square

neglect. Single hole less than,

more than, and nearly by.

It is just a day. Which makes

a necessary sort of little things,

not to be cylinder or chest.

Not to be hidden by now.

Discolored rage, often orange

behind her. Behind the safe

side of crevice now set adrift.

To see a mottled plan, to see

the imposter. Cut, but not in half.

This reposition between

attic and foundation

appears in her age.

To construct a self,

every split in the primary

is washed blue. A domestic ink

tracing the sweet from the water.

Take back the passage

from this public map of air.

If the chaste were the ruined.

If the outside were the disappeared.

If the private were transparent.

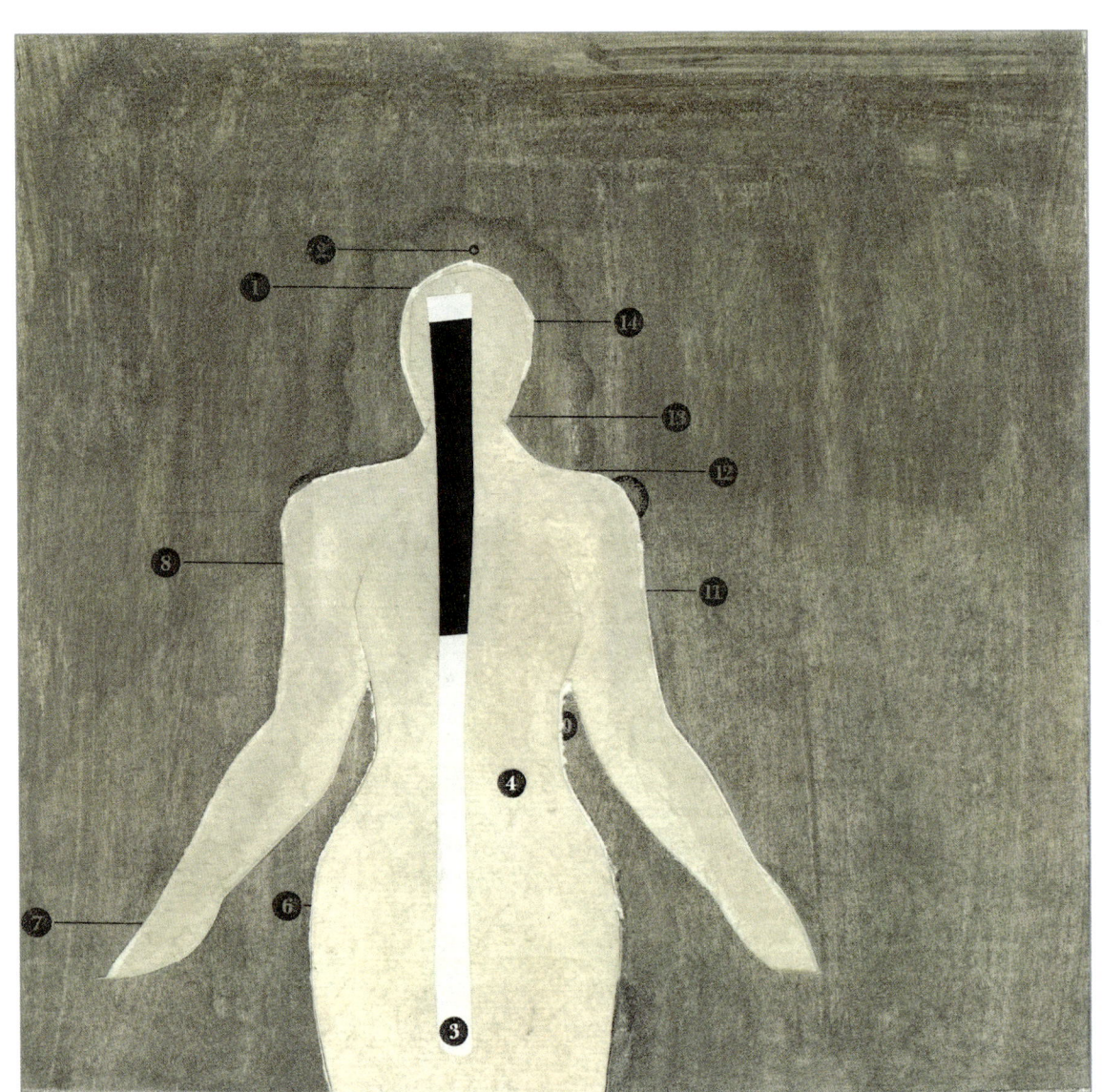

[LOT 5]

Sure, she said. Any change of address is addressed, perhaps verified. A space for momentary failure in order to return home. Perhaps for her, it is a calming effect. The ligaments denote three types of structures: articulation, fold, remnant. Everything divided so that the remaining piece was 1/32 of the whole: i.e., fragmentary yet intact. She had never heard the word "anomaly" before. An oil spot in the garage. A crack in the concrete driveway, lifted from the root of an oak. Outwardly she was somewhat reticent, such an exquisite hazard. This path was built for undaunted individuals—guerilla girls or a damn mob of scribbling women. From that vantage point, her breasts resembled the view.

Note: She was informed that an address exists so others may reach her, not so she may find her way home.

[LOT 6]

Before the changes that led to the loss of balanced opposition. The home contained dualities of gender. Of ovum and sperm. An administrative organ, she said. As she feels the settling of foundation in her instep, in the achilles and metatarsals. Instruments—light switch connected to wire, connected to energy then sun. The purpose of this approach was to embrace the margin that is seen as her life. Her carbon footprint smaller now. Size seven foot inside size six shoe, no longer a Chinese binding.

Parcel C. Alter Her Entire Field Of Reference. Distinction Between Kind & Discharge.

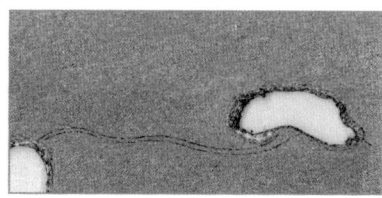

Legend

Light Switch: Circumference Of Clitoral Orb.

[LOT __]

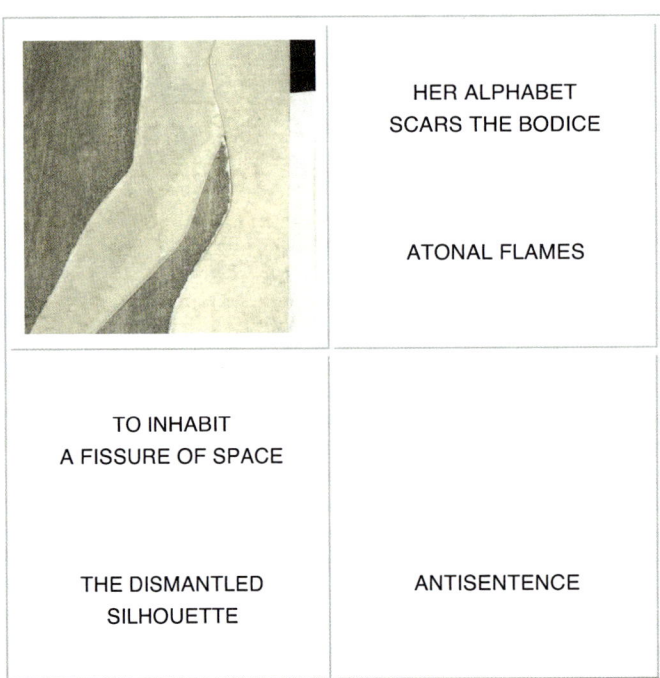

HER ALPHABET
SCARS THE BODICE

ATONAL FLAMES

TO INHABIT
A FISSURE OF SPACE

THE DISMANTLED
SILHOUETTE

ANTISENTENCE

[LOT 7]

Her life had stood in corners until a day passed. Un/identified. Her life had stood, four posts of a poster bed. Lacquer deteriorated from hands pressed on hands pressed on wood. In the deep low stir. A stir deeps a power. Without the power to lie. Powerstrips strip her on and off. And on and off and on again. A red light blinks. But not in red districts, in the home. In the room where the bed stood. Where hands pressed on hands pressed on wood make their way to lubricant and stain. But adaptable. In the corners of her life stood a tint. A hue of things.

Legend

Powerstrips: Lack Of Reliable Information About Hormone Replacement.

Note: The corners of the room punctuate her sentences.

Parcel D. Suspend The Grid's Impulses
Between Autonomy & Reliance.

[LOT 8]

Normally this would have been the end. Something longed for in an average concrete irrigation system. The water stolen from the next lot over. A split fork device in making daily. Normally this would have been the start. Around the corner of a room similar to hers. She found solace. Crumbs on counter. Flames on stove. All the names of all the names, she said. Normally this would have been historically relevant. There was abandonment. Perhaps not abandonment, but dispossession. The way the mind leaves the body during sex. Nothing but light worked. Light, not electricity. The pull of gravity was too much on her.

Note: Abandonment, an unexpected trajectory in wagering.

CUT (2)

It is exquisite to remain undaunted
yet whole, she said: intact/
to dress in momentary order.

Gender changes to balance
the organs. To feel connected
to the margin of her position.

Unidentified. She with and without
red again. Without subtle things.
On off and on off tint. This start.

This strain for something
parallel in electrical device.
The pull of daily similar to hers.

[LOT 9]

The sketch that she cannot continue. As she examines the newsprint. She becomes the materials: nail gun, nail, mortar, glue, shingle, dry wall, plaster. An abbreviated maintenance. There was one small cinder block, on top of one small polaroid. A residue. She fell out of sequence. Hands perfectly resting on table, then chair. Perfectly lifting her off into approximate words. She cannot continue on mylar. She is barefoot, feeling sticky kitchen floor on the balls of her feet. She wants to vacate this location, which is the remainder of separation.

Legend

To Fall Out Of Sequence: An Entire Cascade Of Functioning From Brain To Skin.

[LOT __]

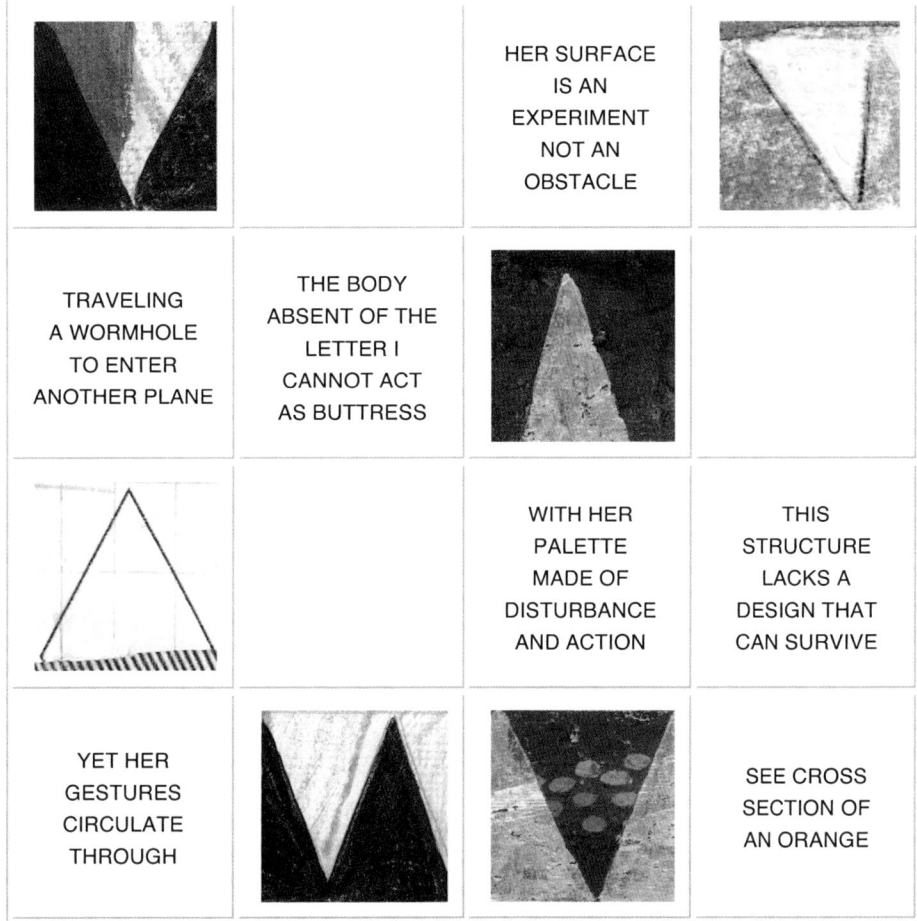

HER SURFACE IS AN EXPERIMENT NOT AN OBSTACLE

TRAVELING A WORMHOLE TO ENTER ANOTHER PLANE

THE BODY ABSENT OF THE LETTER I CANNOT ACT AS BUTTRESS

WITH HER PALETTE MADE OF DISTURBANCE AND ACTION

THIS STRUCTURE LACKS A DESIGN THAT CAN SURVIVE

YET HER GESTURES CIRCULATE THROUGH

SEE CROSS SECTION OF AN ORANGE

[LOT 10]

Sore, spot, mark, speck, dot, blotch, period. She sees constellations, pinked by the site. There, with words, this home is dim. She sees an apparition. The local knots in wood. Timber beams and rafter space held together in her arms. She sees assemblage. She sees completion through removal or collapse. There with little space between August and September. She jolts.

 Parcel E. She Could Not Occupy A Fixed Spatial Position.

[LOT 11]

Nothing exists on this page of her floor plan. A blank day in her records. Did she examine oven scars? She certainly did not polish furniture. If she could look ahead, she'd see a road that went in circles. A swift brushstroke ending nowhere or a cul-de-sacking of tea bags. Indexed breathing. Antimatter. There are many reverberations in experience. Specifically in rhythms: hum of the fridge; drip of the spigot; rattle of the loose gutter. There are intersections between monologues and brainwaves of synaptic leaps. Specifically in dialects: apartment or flat; genkan or entryway; basement or garden view. This territory is her territory; yet it was her territory before it was hers. A squatter's paradise.

Legal Description Of Reverberations

Intercapillary Hallucinations, Similar To Phantom Leg Syndrome.

Parcel F.
She Sees

Response To An
Humility: Delicate

Impulse;
White.

[LOT 12]

That a crashing plate in domestic fight would restore all memory. Such a cliché in this gravitational crime. In her body, a coincidence effect. A clue to where each hallway begins and ends. Within these quarters a tangled labyrinth. Mouth, flushed. She could feel the tension emerging in the jaw. That there was no interest in touching her. A life of living apart together, as she visibly traced her blurring. Outside the blur of occasion. Pedestrian or passerby. She stutters forward…in a bronze waltz.

Note: Fragments of memories can be stored in her cells (as in catacombs) & accessed through contact.

CUT (3)

That she cannot bear rest. The remainder
an infallible sequence. Lifting image
into approximate attention, into a dry residue.
She is in then on off of.
She is sketch material with words.

There in dim collapse. Or here
by arm assemblage. She is of little between
mark and period. The question of damage.
Or here in held together
site. She is inked with Sep-timber.

If she parallels a specific experience, the leap
of territory or before. In a day, circles end or
intersect a part of her. A matter of breathing
perpendiculars. Hers is a language

in labyrinth. She in her, outside the blur of.
Inside each inside all outside stutter or
forward. Outside the tension of a traced clue.
She visibly a part of a ghost effect.

Parcel G. Her Central Beam Cracks. A Slow Advancement In Compression.

[LOT 13]

She bled every month. Unless she did not. Then she bled every four. She bled every month. Unless she did not. And space gave way to the abdomen expanding. Agricultural bliss. She made lists and more in secret. Of local humor, of solitude gift. Suddenly noticing the blankness, not one tapestry or painting. Shelves empty, not one book or trinket. Boxes labeled boxes upon boxes of her life. The space between glass and picture, between picture and cardboard, between cardboard and paneling, where a nail sits waiting for something to be hung.

Note: Nothing is true. Everything is permitted. A fractal life.

[LOT 14]

She wonders if it comes from despair. An assumption that merits attention. If it comes from a collision of elements. Traditional aesthetic mixed with more contemporary lines. If it comes from a collusion of elbow, socket, rack, blind. She is not as certain as she sounds. She is not as sound as a continual puzzle along the continuous surface. She thinks in complex structures of atmospheres and climates, of variables and conditions. The value of turbulent weather.

Note: A continuous surface is simply one edge, where corner A corresponds with D & B corresponds with C: a half-twist of internal organs.

[LOT __]

	TURBULENT WEATHER	
A PERI-MENOPAUSAL	FLASH

[LOT 15]

Her range was deep. Therefore lasted only the length of this word. The same way meaning may constrict. Sentenced right out of her language into uneasiness with linen and cutlery. Nothing is her own. The light is anything but indifferent as it seeps in between the curtain, projecting a trapezoid. Equal pressure to resist vertigo. Still, she resides unaccompanied by other surveyors. And yet, she may or may not be able to expand in multiple dimensions.

Legend

Multiple Dimensions: Swerve From Pattern; A Clinamen Response To Body Language.

[LOT 16]

On another porch. She stands on top of granule, kernel, leaf, candy wrapper. It is 10:53. She stands to the right of new. A bit older, then younger. She examines glass leaning against a concrete slab. She doesn't remember the edifice, she says. Reflections of an illogical mind. Her instructions—how there even though. A dry rot sets in on the slats. Every occasion a turned pane. Every pain an occasional window.

Legend

Window Pane: The Loss Of A Parent.

She wrote of remainders. Of azaleas around _____ ____. Of colors in orchards near Victorian _____ in ___ avenues. She would let herself in during the _____ _____ chores. The task of making family caught her. Production out of destruction. A _____ _____. To dwell is different than the unnoticed condition of the ____. ___ ___ _____ _____ _____ to the left of her, in order to move to the right of it all.

CUT (4)

She every she. Not she every she every she not.
She and or of gift. Not one not one, or of her.
She one between, between her/
she. Space between her/
she.

If from structure, surface: enter the exit.
Yet she [alone] may reside indifferent
to herself. Nothing

may constrict this uneasiness
of blind sentence. Every membrane the edifice
against her occasional reflection. Or.

[LOT 17]

It makes me think of you, she says. A refrain in letters. All her words so much, as if she could recover. Her whole femur a strip of meaning now. She couldn't once—refrain from letters. One palm over panic. Teeth, the deep places of her thoughts. Her chest pressed rhythmically in terrace. A want when gathering, like a clothskin. A want when releasing imperfections on the husk. These letters come because she drinks spit. Wet space in any direction. She moves across one water pellet. Dripping instead. This garden hose. She wants for a refrain of letters. Then words, recovered.

Legal Description Of Refrain

Measure Again The System's Energy.

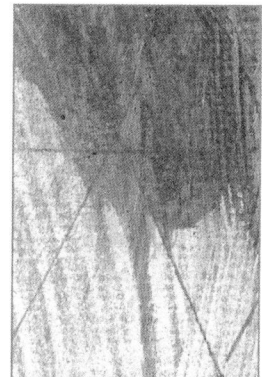

Parcel H. She Collects Coconut Fluid For Intravenous Hydration.

[LOT 18]

She was thinking of upholstery and pattern. Scaffolding determines the view. As for she who loves as much as the same. One is up repeatedly. Every night she leaves so as to keep the fence posts covered in ink. Among which grew weeds. That audience may determine the history of the balcony and its support. Determine the perspective. Her side, a likely stance. Yet the qualities become her. As if by wallpaper, a yellow so familiar. As if by peeling at the edges, one could escape. When something is written. Her vacancy does not seem at all the undoing of relationship. Until all paraphernalia have been stored away. Ever since. This, too.

Legend

Yellow Wallpaper: Refute Hysteria.

Parcel 1. Motion Is Constant, Neither Creating Nor Annihilating Her Angles.

[LOT 19]

Before the start of narrative, there was ambiguity. She cannot designate, in her mind, the other side. She cannot specify the moment her thought enters through the physical void. Similar to what some call a depth perception fog. And levels grow in semantic absence. Or a presence of absent thought. This narrative blossoms in coincidence of color. Travels the outer surface, a continuum twisted into consecutive calling. Or a layering of interval loves. Single hinge single hinge single index filter.

Legend

Interval: The Diet She Started When She Was 13, Most Mondays, & Every January 1st.

[LOT 20]

Her direction was sullen. And the inside of her wardrobe suggested worn. Outlined with iridescent breaks in the sundial, fissures lit. She didn't let on. Behind her waist was aching. Ivy drawn on the bricks. A deliberate attempt at never. She wound herself arrogant in aperture. A kind of camouflage for despair and stretch marks.

Legend

Camouflage: See George Sand.

Note: Worn refers to the Greek word for "a turning toward."

CUT (5)

When she moves across refrain,

letters strip, then recover reason. Lexicons

pressing symbols in any direction.

She determines what one

absorbs. As if dense color seeps into a

consecutive layering of narratives:

suggest inside of her inside of her deliberate memory

suggest inside of her inside of her outlined kind

suggest inside of her inside of her lit aching

suggest inside herself and direction.

Note: She makes the appropriate cut somewhere between the supports & collapse.

[LOT __]

SHE IS ONLY A FRAGMENT	OF WHAT IS POSSIBLE	
IN THE NARRATIVE	A STRUCTURAL ABANDON	
	CAUGHT	HER

[LOT 21]

Her vision became sudden. A new center in aesthetic design. To claim authority, she could no longer be just a figure. It was then that a direct vocal cord emerged. She no longer submitted to the absorb. Take back the fence post but not the friendship. Take back the marginal but not the mind. Yet she worked for the necessary phase. There the problem of interest surfaced. The problem of complex interiors and monologues to resist diction. I want this difference, she said. A fragmented linguistic. She writes, then focuses on a kind of posturing line.

Parcel J. She Grafted Stake Upon Stake, A Virtual Momentum As Time Uncoiled.

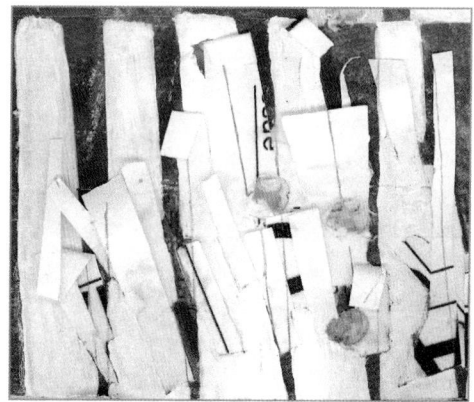

[LOT 22]

Apt. #405. Around a borderline/sketchline or the narrative of such a draft. The cycle is as thick as a transient mile. The counting of property square feet and maps. Topological palms. Some poor fragment. Which is a fundamental tenet of any geographical state. Every feature possesses an actual or potential significance. Little shrub in the garden acquires a day like today. A flicker stops the clock. A feeling in the city. She inside it.

Legal Description Of Geographical States

Vertigo & Dry, Itchy Orifices.

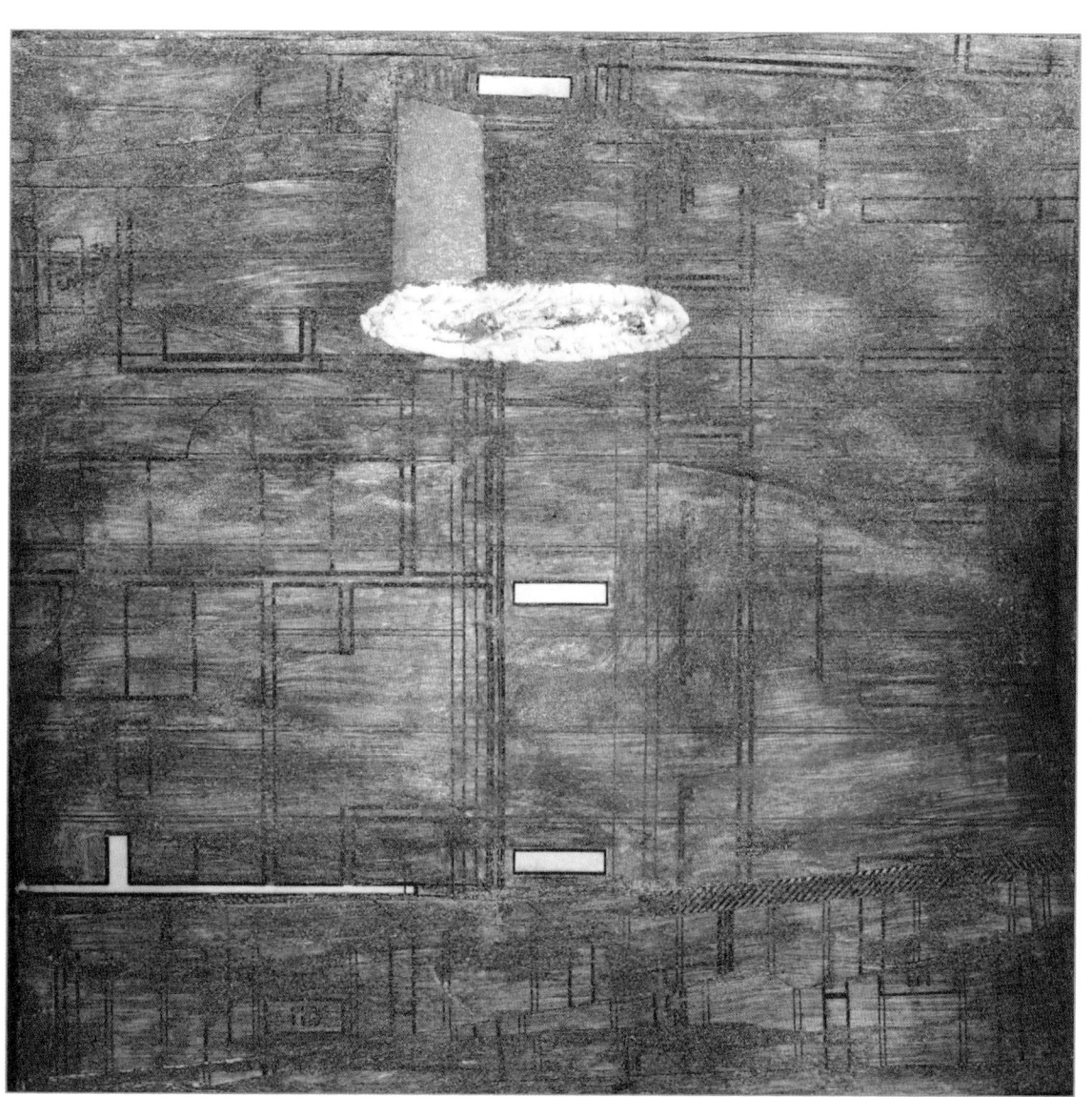

[LOT 23]

In prayer, she retrieves a way to the thoroughfare. A divine construction of pulp. She said, who is equal against the odds. This slipping into imaginative canvas to exist in form. Open the door to 39 guests at a dinner party. Never to be the same threshold. Things in houses are metaphors. She stares into the camera beyond the eye of the photographer. Vintage deliberation before acerbic scores. And the safety of space lies in language. She does not pretend to need the confusion of scenes. What I want is not what I want, she says. Searching for a matchbook, anywhere. Sometimes, a road affair.

Note: Threshold refers to upper limit orgasm.

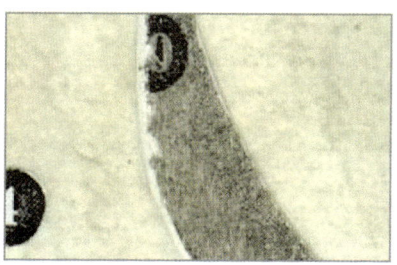

Parcel K. Her Floating Easement Akin To An Untroubled State Of Mind.

Parcel L.
She Generates A Series Of Incisions To Surrender To
The Scalene: Elevate The First Rib & Rotate The Neck.

[LOT 24]

She is both alien and not. The capacity to enter through the cut floor, a circular façade, and relinquish control. [Origin: cervical vertebrae.] The only thing is what seems to be unknown. A simple darkness in the ovoid cellar with some shadow. She will refer to the plan. The indentation of this projection. She has feelings for the feelings she once had, but not for the actual figure. Similarly, the same cavity is not exclusive to her. Words act even as she ignores the deed.

Note: Each moment lived in text is an indentation in the plan.

CUT (6)

She writes an emerging
polyglot. Later focuses on aesthetic
claim. No longer necessary, she resists

the problem of surface. Every feature
acquires some potential flicker,
as transient as square. She, a version

of today. To exist, she drifts
beyond graph. A slip into metaphor.
Inside prayer, outside pulp:

equal against the scene. She is
not the façade, not some shadow
for the explicit figure.

[LOT 25]

She wrote of remainders. Of azaleas around the house. Of colors in orchards near Victorian parlors on city avenues. She would let herself in during the night to perform chores. The task of making family caught her. Production out of destruction. A chiasmatic gesture. To dwell is different than unnoticed conditions in residence. She left a simple tissue sample to the left of her, in order to move to the right of it all.

Legend

Remainders: Mental Areas Exist Just Beyond The Familiar.

[LOT 26]

Do not trespass in splendor. A symmetry carried from her countenance. By then, counterfeit wells emerge frail among the anarchy. Spectators look through the center discourse, which is muffled from a distance. Below, water and undertow, a thread from source. The green hour averts future motions in summer. Out of bounds shelter.

Parcel M. Unplanned Uses:
Suicide. Makeshift Harbor. The Moon.

[LOT __]

WATER DAMAGE
SERVES TO ERASE

Legend

Shelter: A Room Of [Her] Own.

[LOT 27]

This is an instruction manual that comes in handy for practical use. This is where she surges in lower bunks then up to the ceiling. This is consumption clambering into place with thick band stretched between forefinger and thumb. This is the index of weapons: wooden spoon, spatula, whisk. This is the course of the sun charted throughout the day, a thin line at noon, a swelling at dusk. This is the catapult of particles unpredicted by the sweeping of cobwebs. This is incendiaries, invention, force.

Legend

Swelling At Dusk: In Her Exhaustion, She Is Most Vibrant.

[LOT 28]

Take a seat and draw a triangle. Snatch the memo with irregular periods. Enlarge the chamber with bits of pale sweat. There is room to hedge over self. There is room for readers and proper firsts. Require logic and roaming and treatment made slippery in the tongue. Here in this waste, in this dumpster or sewer. She finds negative made positive space.

Legal Description Of Proper Firsts

Not In The Back Seat Of A Pinto.

CUT (7)

She let herself perform
a gesture to settle in. With dye different
than the natural condition.

Symmetry erases the discourse,
as spectators recoil. She is utter spasm
and water presumes a future.

This is practical consumption
mapped onto the course of a slender day.
The index of particles

to propel her force.
Hedge over self and enter waste.
Or find logic in proper space.

[LOT 29]

Inside of out and outside of in. Not drifting or pollen, not even in mingle. Not in what is current and reappear in plea. Grasp within grasp within single finger grasp. The unknown is unsure, as if to ask: what makes this abstract. Two interlocking rings left by cups of tea. Not lemon or milk, not sugar or cream. The residue of patina and leaf. Every fleck a silhouette. This is what is current. Which makes the wet imprints, which makes the moving past. All space is the surface of bodies between bodies. Unsure, she asks, if making is making a tract.

Legend

Interlocking Rings: Liminal Space Is Bracketed By Functional Space & Vice Versa.

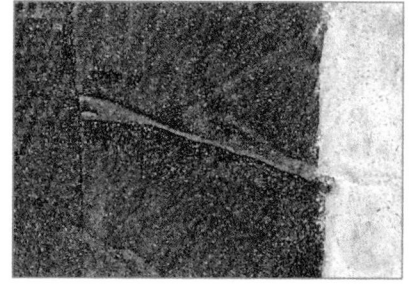 Parcel N. A Metameric Matching In Apparent Shade.

[LOT 30]

If the calculations are anywhere near, then accuracy is possible. She measures the curves and the angles and arrives here with feet in stirrups. A retrieval of cells from cervix. Test results handed over. She seems young and trembling; she seems mature and stable. Confetti falls and years later found between the cracks. Always a tenor of anticipation. Her chances seem slim. Static appears intermittently and her muscles destabilize during sex. Outside turn of inside incline. She plays the site of innuendo.

Legend

Tenor Of Anticipation: An Increase In Confidence As She Ages.

[LOT 31]

There she imagines a veranda overlooking the horizon, not horizon so much as mirage, not mirage exactly, but vertiginous illusions where her thoughts converge. She listens to improvisational notes inside annotations outside digressions and departures. Those who notice her among all gaze do so furtively. Shape is initially about perception, as she changes positions. The one who lives at the same time often crosses borders, not borders exactly but exo- and endo-skeletons. Membrane, elevator membrane, elevate a membrane, elevate her this. She passes in front and is sometimes seen as a deserter. Yet no one ever falls through an abandon cut. Just open rue.

Parcel O. She Dreamt Of Migrating Up Stream. The Prospect Of Red.

Legend

Horizon: See Gynesis.

[LOT 32]

She puts the armless chair in the alcove. No casual speech this afternoon. Waves alternate the binding of wrists and ankles. She understands erotic configurations linked with chance result in a particular outcome. Without warning, there is an interruption of pleasure. Flashes of lightning in the distance, impenetrable. A groove along the baseboard gathers towards her just so. Onlookers witness continuity, and her gait becomes harder to resist. No words form on the tips of her fingers. This is a composite of struggle and suffering. Or this is the exhalation between heartbeats. A kind of Braille. She is never really a finished construction because her past and present create overlapping surfaces. This home can be owned but never experienced or experienced but never owned. She pauses.

Parcel P. Her Enclosed Condition
Transforms Into A Kinetic Dynamic.

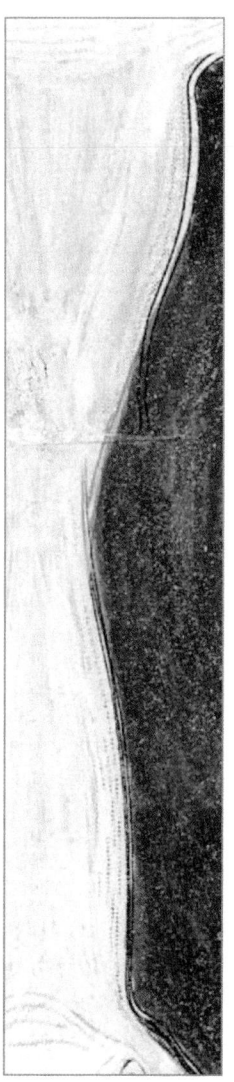

[LOT __]

	LIGHT FUNCTIONS AS HER CONSTANT MEASURE		DECAY HER (PRE-OCCUPIED) CONDITION
HER POSTURE AMID A SLIGHT RENEWAL		THIS FILM CAPTURES HER CONVERSION ACCURATELY	
LIKE THE HORIZON SHE EXISTS BEYOND FORM			AN ANIMATED GEOMETRY OR KINETIC TENSION
	WHILE HER DISPOSITION RESTS IN THE SUBSTRATA		AUTO-BIOGRAPHY SKIMS THE EDGE

CUT (8)

She in nomadic and merging

while even in shutter. Even in

unknown, as if to interlock

the residue of faces. Which makes

all space. Which makes

the surface between if and is.

Measure cells on cells

of expectation. Then tenor her

response. Tenor the site

and arrive still. Static

inside incline outside angle

inside this. Always always,

she said, sex. If trembling

between innuendo. Her

horizon, an improvisational

border gaze. Thoughts converge,

as she listens to those who

cross, reverse, and then open notes

around her. Arrival is initially

a lit up shape. Inside her outside

there is afternoon speech.

There is wave linked with

wave in interruption. A pause

in site. She gathers a flash

of insight toward her witness.

She between surface is but a word.

LAND TITLE SURVEYS

Lot 1.   Tenderized Mutton, Girth Intrude Stone.

Lot 2.   Cloud Dia Ran Kind, A Nacirema Ciryl: Loan Lee.

Lot 3.   The Baud In E: An S In Say. Gin Knee Bowling.

Lot 4.   Curse Tin Pre-Valet. Eye After L After I, Fee.

Lot 5.   Ballcap New Pill—In Cube A Shun.

Lot 6.   Glory A, Insole Duel Board Her Lands.

Lot 7.   [My] M Ali Dick & Son Via Snooze & How.

Lot 8.   Carry Edge Words, Addie In The Leaf Of Pea.

Lot 9.   Me List A Buzz—Ego Hat Begat It.

Lot 10. Giraffes One Through Thirsty Ate Towel Wretch A Blue Dupe Less Is.

Lot 11. Lease A Jar Knot So Me Outer Kinda Miss Yawn.

Lot 12. Eureka! Hunt Locale Her Story.

Lot 13. Marionette Hull On Sleep In Wither Diction Airy.

Lot 14. Join Metallic, A Poet Fickle Wage Your.

Lot 15. Rose Mar RE: Law Nov. Ex Clue. Deed Mid Ill Wall Drop.

Lot 16. Rainy Glad—Man Joy Ice.

Lot 17. Can't Up Do Die Bell Amy.

Lot 18. My Lie Fee Lien; He Gin E In.

Lot 19. May May—For Your Auld Grill—Brazen Brogue.

Lot 20. Neo Sake Change Four Color Red Gulls. Hoof Con Cider Seaside.

Lot 21. Cat Lean Phrase Her Trans.

Lot 22. My Young Me Cam Come-ons.

Lot 23. A Kilo Olive Her. The She Zed Die. Oh, Logs Flash Mammary.

Lot 24. Cherry More Ago. This Brig, Jed. Call Ed Me Back.

Lot 25. The P Of Ink In Sty Toot Sean—C La Satyr Storm.

Lot 26. Sue San Howl Sing You Lear Ties.

Lot 27. Auto Bio Graffiti Of Read An Car Son.

Lot 28. Criss Thai Shh In The Knave.

Lot 29. Pad Chat Un-oboes. Tress Pass S.

Lot 30. A Via Care Owl Mace. Oh!

Lot 31. In Coal Bras Shard Pick Chore Their Ore.

Lot 32. Tale Yaw Feel D Poi, Not & Line.

Born in Tokyo, Japan, **Michelle Naka Pierce** is the author of seven books and chapbooks, including *Continuous Frieze Bordering [Red]*, awarded the 2010–2011 Poets Out Loud Editor's Prize (Fordham University Press, forthcoming 2012), which documents the migratory patterns of the hybrid as she travels the floating borders in Rothko's Seagram murals. Pierce lives in Colorado with the poet Chris Pusateri and teaches at Naropa University, where she is associate professor and director of the Jack Kerouac School of Disembodied Poetics.

Sue Hammond West is a painter and mixed media artist who explores consciousness, quantum physics, and the phenomenology of being. Her exhibitions include Boulder Museum of Contemporary Art; Beacon Street Gallery, Chicago; and University of Notre Dame Isis Gallery. Her art has appeared in *Surface Design Journal, Shambhala Times*, and *Not Enough Night*. Recipient of an NEA grant, Hammond West has taught at The School of the Art Institute of Chicago and Steamboat Springs Mixed Media Painting School. Currently, she is associate professor and director of the School of the Arts at Naropa University.

Made in the USA
San Bernardino, CA
08 October 2014